*Lives based on
having are less free
than lives based either
on doing or being.*

William James

# 101 ways to simplify your life

### Candy Paull

Brentwood, Tennessee

*No one can be*
*making much of*
*his life who has*
*not a very definite*
*conception of what*
*he is living for.*

Henry Drummond

# Contents

# Contents continued...

# Introduction

*101 Ways to Simplify Your Life* offers practical advice that can help you clear both outer and inner clutter and can encourage you to order your priorities around what matters most. Outward actions like cleaning a closet, making do with less, and creating simple entertainment are balanced with inner choices that help you remember what is important and meaningful to you. As you simplify, you make room for personal transformation and spiritual growth.

Choosing simplicity gives much more than it takes away, for it leads to a life of freedom, peace, and joy. May *101 Ways to Simplify Your Life* help you focus on the essentials, enhance your daily life, and encourage you to nurture a deeper relationship with God.

Let us go on in simplicity of heart, in peace and joy, which are the fruits of the Holy Spirit.

François Fénelon

*A pretentious, showy life is an empty life; a plain and simple life is a full life.*

Proverbs 13:7 MSG

# #1

## Jump Off the Merry-Go-Round

Simplifying your life sounds like an impossible dream in a hectic, over-worked, overscheduled world. The endless whirl of activities and demands of modern living often feel like an out-of-control merry-go-round, spinning you in circles and taking you nowhere fast.

You don't have to stay on the merry-go-round. Your decision to step off and start in another direction is all it takes. Begin by making one small change in your life: clear some clutter, make more space in your calendar, and spend more time in prayer and meditation. Ask God to show you ways to simplify and change the direction of your life.

jump

*There are many activities I must cut out simply because I desire to excel in my pursuit after God and holiness.*

Wendell W. Price

≫ Pray each morning for God's wisdom on how you can best use your time that day.

# #2

## Honor Simple Truths

*The entrance of Your words gives light; it gives understanding to the simple.*

Psalm 119:130 NKJV

honor

You were taught these simple truths when you were a child: Say thank you. Share your toys. Be kind to others. Trust God. Take frequent naps. Be content with what you have.

This homespun heart-wisdom still applies, no matter how sophisticated your adult world seems to be: Give thanks to God for the blessings you have received. Share your wealth with others, and you'll have true riches. Lend a helping hand to create a warm-hearted community. Do what's right and follow God's ways. Get enough rest. Savor what you have in this moment. Honor these simple truths and you will be blessed.

≫ Take time to enjoy a conversation with someone you admire. Ask what simple truths have guided him or her through life.

# #3

## Remember That Less Can Be More

When asked how he carved beautiful elephants from blocks of stone, a famous Indian sculptor replied that he just chipped away everything that wasn't an elephant. Look at what you do and what you own. Ask yourself, "Is this essential? Does this thing or activity enhance my life? Is this necessary, or is it clutter that hinders and hampers me?"

Pruning overgrown bushes allows more light into a house. Having less of what you don't want frees you to concentrate more on what you do want. Clear time in your calendar for prayer and planning. Create space in your surroundings by eliminating that which no longer serves you.

less

> *Every time you make a choice you are turning the central part of you, the part that chooses, into something a little different than it was before.*
>
> C. S. Lewis

>> Evaluate your possessions and activities. Decide what you need to eliminate so you are free to focus on what's most essential and meaningful to you.

# #4

## Choose Uplifting Entertainment

> *You'll do best by filling your minds and meditating on things true, noble, reputable, authentic, compelling, gracious — the best, not the worst; the beautiful, not the ugly; things to praise, not things to curse.*
>
> Philippians 4:8 MSG

choose

Simplify your life by making different entertainment choices. Choosing entertainment alternatives that lift your spirits and encourage you to be a better person will give you extra energy and enhance your spiritual life. Your entertainment choices color your mood and affect your attitude. Inspiring entertainment makes you feel better about life.

When you want to watch something on TV, look for programs that inform as well as entertain. Choose uplifting movies with great stories instead of movies with thin plot lines and violent special effects. Better yet, get away from passive entertainment altogether and create your own fun.

>> Instead of watching television or playing computer games, read a good book, get together with friends, or go for a walk in nature.

# #5

## Spend Reflective Time Alone

A workable strategy for remaining productive over the long haul is to balance busy times with downtime. Create space in your schedule for personal reflection, time to think about life. Let go of the schedules and agendas of the day. Allow yourself some time to daydream, to mull over the events of the day, and to review your priorities.

Set aside regular times for contemplation and prayer. Quieting your heart and listening to God allows you to access wisdom from above. Time taken for reflection refreshes your spirit, allowing you to step back and see the larger picture.

alone

> *Contemplation is nothing else but a secret, peaceful, and loving infusion of God, which, if admitted, will set the soul on fire with the Spirit of love.*
>
> Saint John of the Cross

≫ Brew a cup of coffee or tea. As you sip its comforting warmth, take a few moments to sit quietly and reflect on what is important to you.

# #6

## Enjoy What You Have

*Better a little with the fear of the LORD than great wealth with turmoil.*

Proverbs 15:16 NIV

enjoy

Your tool chest may be overflowing, but it would be great to have that new gadget advertised on TV. Your closet may be full of clothes, but the department store offers such a bright array of new fashions. The appetite for *new!* and *improved!* can blind you to what you already have.

Appreciate what you have now. Use your tools to create a fun project. Decide to enjoy clothes you own but never wear. Appreciate the life you have, too. Enjoy your home, your friends, and your family. Be thankful for the gifts God has given you, and trust that you have enough right now.

>> Learn to differentiate between needs and wants. Instead of thinking about what you don't have, thank God for what you do have.

# #7

## Lend a Helping Hand

*help*

In frontier days, people gathered together to help one another. Quilting bees and barn raisings and threshing crews were not only necessary for survival, but they built community and friendships as well. Your willingness to lend a helping hand to others can create a caring community that will support you, too.

A supportive community brings you closer to simpler times, when neighbor depended on neighbor and friendships were forged by working together for the common good. The law of sowing and reaping says that you will receive what you are willing to give. Work together, and you'll discover that many hands make light work.

> *Carry each other's burdens, and in this way you will fulfill the law of Christ.*
>
> Galatians 6:2 NIV

>> Resolve to create a community of giving and receiving. Start by helping a friend or neighbor, and don't be shy about asking for help in return.

# #8

## Reduce Your Spending

> *It's good to have money and the things that money can buy, but it's good, too, to check up once in a while and make sure that you haven't lost the things that money can't buy.*
>
> George Horace Lorimer

**reduce**

Reducing the amount of money that goes out every month gives you more options and more time. When you cut back on expenses, avoid unnecessary expenditures, and set aside the money you would have spent, then you have extra money to do the things you really want to do.

How you spend your money reveals your true priorities. Spending less means less time spent shopping and taking care of things you buy. Instead of using your time for the things money can buy, you can concentrate on enjoying the things that money can't buy, including time for family, friends, and spiritual pursuits.

>> Be aware of where your money goes. Create a general budget and track your spending. Cut back on extras and make do with what you have.

# #9

## Take a Deep Breath

Deep breathing is a simple way to relieve stress and tension. Shallow breathing creates a feeling of tightness and constriction, putting you into a fight-or-flight mode. Deep breathing, how-ever, relaxes and slows you down.

Your body, entwined with mind and spirit, is wonderfully made by God. When you make gentle physical adjustments, like taking several deep breaths, you enjoy a corresponding mental and spiritual adjustment. As you open your lungs to receive the breath of life, allow the oxygenating energy to fill your entire body. As you release your breath in a deep exhale, let go of tension and constriction.

breath

> *Take one long breath to help you relax and relieve tension and stress. Deep breathing has a positive, long-range impact on your health.*
>
> Zig Ziglar

>> Use daily deep breathing exercises as an opportunity to pray. Breathe in the love of God. Exhale and let go of that which no longer serves you.

# #10
## Select Wisely

> *If any of you lacks wisdom, let him ask of God, who gives to all liberally and without reproach, and it will be given to him.*
>
> James 1:5 NKJV

select

When you make wise choices, you don't have to backtrack or expend energy correcting mistakes. Life becomes less complicated, because you aren't taking unnecessary detours or trying to rebuild bridges you burned.

How do you learn to make better decisions and select more wisely? Taking time to weigh the pros and cons of a choice is one way. Another way is to profit from experience, your own or others'. Becoming still before God and asking for guidance in your decisions is a powerful way to find wisdom when you need it. Before you make any important decision, spend time in prayer and listen for God's wisdom.

≫ The next time you have a decision to make, ask for God's guidance so that you can make the best choice for all concerned.

# #11

## Rescue Discarded Treasures

One man's trash is another man's treasure. Hunt for treasure at yard sales, flea markets, Goodwill, or other places that recycle what others can no longer use. Even if your bargain used dresser doesn't turn out to be a valuable antique in disguise, you will have the pleasure of finding new uses for an old and beloved belonging—the essence of simple living.

Rescuing discarded treasures mirrors what God does with your life. He sees the value in what others disregard. Instead of discarding that which is still useful, he knows the quality and worth that lies beneath the scratched surface.

rescue

*The kingdom of heaven is like treasure hidden in a field. When a man found it, he hid it again, and then in his joy went and sold all he had and bought that field.*

Matthew 13:44 NIV

>> Check out yard sales and flea markets for unique items and unexpected bargains. You may discover a hidden treasure that no one else sees.

# #12

## Focus on Quality, Not Quantity

> *Get wisdom—it's worth more than money; choose insight over income every time.*
>
> Proverbs 16:16 MSG

quality

Just because something is cheaper by the dozen doesn't mean that you need a dozen of whatever it is. If you have a choice between several cheap items or one quality item for the same price, don't be fooled into thinking that quantity makes up for quality. One beautifully made piece of clothing will serve you better than five cheaper items of lesser quality.

Make wise choices that simplify your life by focusing on quality instead of quantity—in relationships as well as in material things. And don't forget to ask God to help you discern true quality in every situation you encounter.

>> Buy a fine-quality tool that will serve you dependably for many years instead of an inexpensive one of inferior workmanship that will fall apart after a few uses.

# #13

## Discover the Delights of Poetry

The simple life is not only about money and things. It's about how you spend your time and feed your spirit. One of the great pleasures of the life well-lived is the enjoyment of poetry.

Poetry has its practical side. It expands your understanding and introduces you to the best thoughts of some of the greatest writers of all time. A great poem lifts your spirit, for it is wisdom distilled in the art of making words play together and ideas dance in the mind. Whether you enjoy a classic poem or meditate on a psalm, poetry will enrich your life.

poetry

> *Poetry is the art of uniting pleasure with truth by calling imagination to the help of reason.*
>
> Samuel Johnson

>> Enjoy anthologies of poetry. *A Treasury of Great Poems: An Inspiring Collection of the Best-Loved, Most Moving Verse in the English Language,* compiled by Louis Untermeyer, is a wonderful collection.

# #14

## Enjoy Seasonal Abundance

*For everything there is a season, and a time for every matter under heaven.*

Ecclesiastes 3:1 NRSV

enjoy

Cardboard-flavored winter supermarket tomatoes can never duplicate summer ripe tomatoes. When fruits and vegetables are in season, they deliver fabulous flavor at the lowest prices. So it is also with life.

Savoring seasonal abundance is an easy way to enjoy life every day of the year. Instead of going on expensive vacations to distant climates, enjoy an hour or two celebrating the seasons at home. Enjoy fruit when it's at its peak, be thankful in whatever weather a day offers, stop and smell the roses, and give thanks for the small joys of living simply in God's seasonal abundance.

≫ Enjoy simple seasonal celebrations: gather fall leaves, build a snowman, pick a spring bouquet, light sparklers, have a summer picnic, visit a farmers' market.

# #15

## Recharge Your Spiritual Batteries

recharge

You expend energy every day. Work demands your best effort, people need your attention, and chores pile up like autumn leaves. You dream of a simpler life, but the complications of everyday living get in the way.

Though you can't escape to a deserted tropical island, you can find an oasis of calm and comfort in the presence of God. Realize that taking time to recharge your spiritual batteries will help you better cope with the challenges of life. Set aside some time each day to bask in God's love and allow him to refill your reservoir of faith and strength.

*Because so many people were coming and going that they did not even have a chance to eat, [Jesus] said to [his disciples], "Come with me by yourselves to a quiet place and get some rest."*

Mark 6:31 NIV

≫ Take time out from your busy life to enjoy God's presence. Retreat from the world for a few moments of prayer, spiritual reading, or meditation.

begin

# 101 ways to

share

clear

choose

balance

# simplify your life

appreciate

gather

reduce

# #16

## Simplify Your Surroundings

> *We shape our dwellings, and afterwards our dwellings shape us.*
>
> Sir Winston Churchill

simplify

One particularly effective way to make your life simpler is to clear your living space of clutter to create an atmosphere of peaceful calm instead of chaos and disorder. As you clean and clear, decide what you want to keep and where you want to keep it. Invest in good storage. There are clever, inexpensive storage alternatives available.

Simple surroundings take advantage of clean lines and natural beauty. Instead of a welter of small knickknacks, consider replacing them with an elegant bonsai plant or a single treasured antique artistically displayed. Timeless simplicity soothes the spirit and creates an oasis of calm in a busy life.

>> Follow these simple guidelines for keeping clutter under control: If you take it out, put it back. If you open it up, close it. If you throw it down, pick it up.

# #17

## Clear Out Emotional Clutter

Just as clearing clutter in your living space calms and soothes you, so clearing emotional clutter helps you live life more freely from the heart. Emotional clutter includes the ego agendas that trip you up in your relationships. Galatians 5:19–21 lists toxic emotions of the lower nature that include hatred, discord, rage, jealousy, and envy.

Verses 22 and 23 offer the contrast of the fruit of the Spirit: love, joy, peace, patience, kindness, goodness, faithfulness, gentleness, and self-control. As you allow God to clear your emotional clutter, you'll begin to experience more of the sweet serenity that comes through the fruit of the Spirit.

clear

> *He who reigns within himself and rules his passions, desires, and fears is more than a king.*
>
> John Milton

≫ When you are hurting, take your emotions of fear, anger, anxiety, and frustration to God. Write your prayers and feelings in a journal.

# #18

## Use a Bible-Reading Plan

*Your word is a lamp for my feet and a light for my path.*

Psalm 119:105 NLT

plan

You may have the best intentions to do spiritual reading on a regular basis. But unless you have a plan, it's easy to get off track. Instead of dabbling here and there in your reading, take advantage of the many daily devotional books and Bible reading plans available.

You can read the Bible through in a year, using a reading plan or a Bible designed with daily reading in mind. There are excellent devotionals available that offer thoughts on a particular subject, such as prayer. Some devotionals are compilations of the best writing of one author. Having a plan simplifies your reading and helps you stay consistent.

≫ Start your new year right with a plan to read sections of the Bible on a regular and orderly basis.

# #19

## Ask for Help

ask

You may believe that you should be strong and self-sufficient all the time and that you are weak and shameful if you ask for help. But in God's economy, it takes both giving and receiving to create a balanced life. When you give too much without receiving, you become exhausted and depleted.

Simplify your life by learning to receive as well as to give. Without guilt or shame, ask for help when you need it. Just as you have delighted in helping others, so allow others to delight in helping you. Put false pride aside, and allow God to send you his ministering angels.

*God has given us two hands—one to receive with and the other to give with. We are not cisterns made for hoarding; we are channels made for sharing.*

Billy Graham

≫ When you are feeling overwhelmed, ask God for help. Remember that receiving is as important as giving, and allow others to help you.

# #20

## Be Original, Not Mass-Produced

> *I will praise You, for I am fearfully and wonderfully made; marvelous are Your works, and that my soul knows very well.*
>
> Psalm 139:14 NKJV

original

You are unique—God created you, and you are here in this time and this place to bring your special gifts to the world. It's simpler to be authentic, for then you make choices that reflect who you really are.

Resolve to honor the unique gifts God gave you. While others may have gifts and talents you admire, thinking poorly of yourself will not make you a better person. Know your strengths and your abilities and consider how you can best use them for God. Rejoice that you are an original—not a mass-produced imitation of someone else.

≫ Become aware of the ways you may tell yourself that you're not good enough. Replace these thoughts with the truth that you are precious in God's eyes.

# #21

## Take Longer to Do Less

With today's emphasis on productivity and multitasking, you can drive yourself into a frenzy trying to do everything all at once. But God didn't create you to be a 24/7 machine. You are a spiritual being, and you need to honor the spiritual aspects of your life and work.

More and faster can sometimes be counterproductive. You may end up feeling overwhelmed. Instead of trying to squeeze more tasks into fewer moments, decide that for today you'll do a little less and take more time to enjoy what you have chosen to do. You'll feel less rushed and will clarify and simplify your priorities.

l o n g e r

> *Only eternal values can give meaning to temporal ones. Time must be the servant of eternity.*
>
> Erwin W. Lutzer

≫ Instead of multitasking, give yourself wholeheartedly to one activity at a time. Enjoy the satisfaction of completing one meaningful task without interruption.

# #22

## Give Others Your Undivided Attention

*Don't think only about your own affairs, but be interested in others, too, and what they are doing.*

Philippians 2:4 NLT

g i v e

When you concentrate on one thing at a time, you give your best self to your endeavors. This holds true in your relationships as well as in your work. Honor other people as spiritual beings who are beloved by God. Enjoy being with them. Be fully present and fully attentive, aware of how precious and unique each person is.

Choosing to pay attention simplifies your conversational priorities. Instead of thinking about what you want to say, focus on the other person. This will free you to really listen to what that person is saying. Undivided attention means an undistracted mind, and it helps you keep your heart open and compassionate.

≫ The next time you are conversing with other people, give them your full attention. Listen closely to what they have to say.

# #23

## Live with What You Love

That ugly lamp was a mistake when you bought it, and it hasn't improved with time. An uncomfortable chair is a family heirloom, but you can never bring yourself to sit in it. It's time to clear your home of things you don't like.

Fill the rooms with things you love instead. You will be happier and more peaceful when you do. Just as comfortable and flattering clothing makes you feel your best, so beauty and order create an elegant simplicity in your home. Before you bring anything into your home, ask yourself, "Is this beautiful? Is it useful? Do I love it?"

love

*Have nothing in your homes that you do not know to be useful and believe to be beautiful.*

William Morris

>> Start with one room in your home: weed out the clutter and leave only those things that feel useful or beautiful to you.

# #24
## Look at the Big Picture

> *We know that God causes all things to work together for good to those who love God, to those who are called according to His purpose.*
>
> **Romans 8:28** NASB

picture

Look at your life from God's perspective. Instead of getting caught up in details and problems, look at the big picture. Viewed from a distance, irritations look small and petty, while eternal things, like love, take on greater importance.

When you are having a disagreement with a friend, step back and look at him or her through a more generous lens. Instead of magnifying faults, see the simple truth: this person means a great deal to you, or you wouldn't care about this situation. Place each situation in the hands of God, who promises to work all things together for good.

>> Resolve to view your troubles from God's perspective. Ask God to help you discover the positive in seemingly negative situations.

# #25

## Don't Confuse Things with Happiness

confuse

It feels wonderful after you buy something you really want—for a while. But it doesn't take long for the thrill to subside and be replaced by the desire for another material object. Things break, wear out, or are taken for granted. If you frequently find yourself thinking, *I'll be happy when I get this thing,* choose instead to place your happiness in God's hands.

Happiness comes from the heart. You will be less tempted to fill your life with clutter when you concentrate on higher priorities such as love, service, and authentic self-expression. Trust God to satisfy your deepest needs. Then things will be in their proper place.

> *Lives based on having are less free than lives based either on doing or being.*
>
> William James

>> Do something to make someone else happy. Enjoy the simple pleasures of giving a gift, taking someone out to lunch, meeting a need, or just spending quality time together.

# #26

## Give Something Away

*If you give, you will receive. Your gift will return to you in full measure, pressed down, shaken together to make room for more, and running over. Whatever measure you use in giving—large or small—it will be used to measure what is given back to you.*

Luke 6:38 NLT

A generous heart finds simple joy in giving. By sharing good things with others, you loosen your tight grip on the things that perish and place them in God's hands instead. As you give, you will receive.

Buy a gift that you would enjoy receiving, or share something that has held meaning for you. Develop a spirit of generosity by giving something away. Give your best, not a discard. Give the gift of yourself, along with the object you give away. Giving in this generous spirit frees God to give you more, for he knows you can be trusted with his good gifts.

≫ Cultivate a spirit of generosity by giving away something you have enjoyed so that someone else may enjoy it too.

# #27

## Value Who You Are

Life is freer and simpler when you learn to value who you are, instead of measuring your worth by what you do, how much you own, or how many credentials you've amassed. There is something unchanging and beautiful about the essential you, the person God sees when he looks into your heart.

The essential you comes from a place of love. Childlike wonder and unwavering faith are in your deepest heart of hearts. Things turn to dust, jobs end, and your body grows older. But nothing can separate the essential you from the love of God, the One who values who you are.

value

> *My business is not to remake myself, but make the absolute best of what God made.*
>
> Robert Browning

≫ Find a wonderful picture of yourself when you were in elementary school. Frame it and display it to remind yourself of who you are and where you've come from.

# #28

## Cultivate Inner Wisdom

*Come here and listen to me! I'll pour out the spirit of wisdom upon you and make you wise.*

Proverbs 1:23 NLT

wisdom

You may have a string of degrees and be smart as a whip. But that doesn't make you wise. Wisdom comes with experience and through the cultivation of a deeper relationship with God. Inner wisdom helps you navigate the twists and turns of life, simplifying difficult problems with spiritual truth.

Cultivate inner wisdom by making your spiritual life a priority. Spend time in prayer, study, and worship. Make time for spiritual reading. Meditate on Scripture and on wise words from others who have traveled down the spiritual path. Listen to God, and he will bring you the wisdom you desire.

≫ Pray the words of Scripture to deepen your spiritual life and cultivate inner simplicity. Psalm 23 and Psalm 51 are good places to start.

# #29

## Nourish Body and Soul

Slow down and enjoy the food you eat. The simple life is lived at a more measured pace, and gobbling your food or rushing through fast-food meals neither nurtures your body nor honors your soul.

Linger over a leisurely meal that's delicious and nourishing. Savor every bite, and let mealtimes be times of refreshment and renewal. Enjoy a relaxed conversation over a cup of herbal tea with a friend. Let meals become a soulful event, where the loved ones gather together and appreciate the blessings of God. Then the simple act of eating will nourish your soul as well as your body.

nourish

> *Healthy prodding and stirring of the soil should produce, not only nourishing fruit for the body, but also most nourishable food for the mind.*
>
> Saint Augustine

>> Choose a meal this week to eat slowly and with intention. Prepare nourishing and delicious dishes and give yourself time to savor them.

# #30

## Appreciate the Little Things

> *I will praise the LORD God with a song and a thankful heart.*
>
> Psalm 69:30 CEV

little

The smell of coffee brewing in the morning. A hug and a kiss before you leave for work. The perky daisy that sits proudly in a vase on your desk. A smile and hello from a friend. Taking your shoes off and relaxing for a few minutes after a long day. The sound of crickets outside as you fall asleep on a summer night.

Small things make up the simple life. Big events are few and far between. But the little things make life worth living. Appreciate each gift and acknowledge that it comes from the hand of God.

>> Think about five little things you love about your life, and thank God for them.

# #31

## Emphasize Style over Fashion

Fashion dates you, but style is timeless. Fashion is the miniskirt or the mohawk you sported in high school. Style is the way you approach life as an adult. Instead of cluttering your closet with trendy clothes that are here today and nowhere tomorrow, enjoy a few classic pieces that take you through the years.

Style is about simplicity and being comfortable in your own skin. The man or woman of style doesn't need to impress. Style is who you are, not just what you wear. Let your style come not from current trends but from the inner person who loves life and trusts in God.

style

> *Cheerfulness and content are great beautifiers, and are famous preservers of good looks.*
>
> Charles Dickens

≫ The next time you go shopping, choose well-made classic clothes that you'll enjoy for years instead of trendy items that will be outdated next season.

decide

# 101 ways to

invest

experience

read

resolve

# simplify your life

honor

enjoy

see

# #32

## Be More Flexible

> [Jesus] said, "I've come to change everything, turn everything rightside up."
>
> Luke 12:50 MSG

flexible

Life is too large to control. Rigid belief systems and inflexible attitudes cannot stop the flow of change. Instead of trying to contain life—and God—in the little box of your own experience, open your heart to receive new ideas and a larger understanding of who you are and what God wants to do in your life.

Welcome growth and change by becoming more flexible in your attitudes and actions. Try something you've never tried before. Stretch yourself by learning something new. Be open to other opinions and ideas. Life is easier and much more fun when you relax and enjoy the unexpected.

≫ Write your thoughts about situations you wish you could control. Then take time to pray about them and release them to God.

# #33

## Watch the Grass Grow

If you worry too much about productivity, about being busy and important, you need a time-out to find a brighter and wider perspective. Go outdoors and enjoy the freedom of being one of God's creatures in creation. In God's world there is room for both the busy bee and the quiet, cud-chewing cow.

Life gains a certain space and graciousness when you practice the gentle art of doing nothing. Go ahead, you have permission to just "be." Watch the grass grow. Feel the wind on your face. Rejoice in creation. Remember that you are a human being, not a human doing.

g r o w

> *There is such a thing as sacred idleness, the cultivation of which is now fearfully neglected.*
>
> George MacDonald

≫ Enjoy a few minutes of quiet leisure today. Let your mind wander, watch passing clouds, and rest. Then return to your tasks refreshed.

# #34

## Bring Nature Indoors

> *Ask the earth and the sea, the plains and the mountains, the sky and the clouds, the stars and the sun, the fish and the animals, and all of them will say, "We are beautiful because God made us."*
>
> Saint Augustine

nature

You don't need fancy or expensive things to beautify your home and give you pleasure. Stones found in a riverbed, an elegantly curved conch shell, or a colorful bouquet of spring flowers can bring nature indoors, offering a seasonal selection of color and variety for little or no cost.

Reconnecting to the rhythms of nature helps you slow down and connect to the elemental rhythms inside yourself. Paper-white narcissus blooming on a winter window sill remind you of God's seasons of blossom in your life. The restful green of a houseplant makes a corner of your home more welcoming.

>> Go for a walk in nature and bring back something beautiful to enjoy inside: a handful of fall leaves, intriguing rocks, a feather you found by the roadside.

# #35

## Make Sundays Special

In the Bible, the Sabbath is a day of rest. It gives God's people a time away from the business of life for renewal and refreshment. An old-fashioned Sunday in the American South offered a time for worship, a time for play, and a time to feast with the family around a bountiful table.

Once a week, declare a Sabbath. Let this break in the rhythm of your week be a time for both play and worship, rest and fellowship. Setting aside one day a week for renewal will energize you for the workweek ahead. Sabbath is a simple prescription for a happier life.

Sunday

> *The LORD will guide you continually, and satisfy your soul in drought, and strengthen your bones; you shall be like a watered garden, and like a spring of water, whose waters do not fail.*
>
> Isaiah 58:11 NKJV

>> Make this Sunday a true day of rest by taking time to relax, enjoy being with family, and spend quiet moments alone with God.

# #36

## Grow Your Soul by Gardening

> *It is good to live, and all the more good to live in a garden.*
>
> Gertrude Jekyll

grow

You can't return to the perfect innocence of the Garden of Eden, but you can create a corner of Eden in a home garden. Whether you have extensive gardens with fruit trees and a host of flowers, fruits, and vegetables, or just a pot or two of herbs and flowers on an apartment deck, growing green things fills the heart with a simple, earthy satisfaction.

As you get your hands in the good earth, pulling weeds, pruning, and ordering your garden, you can weed and sort through your problems, too. Try a little inexpensive garden therapy to bring a clearer perspective on life.

>> Restore your soul and replenish your spirit by tending a garden. Grow herbs in pots, cultivate a rose, or plant a vegetable garden.

# #37

## Spend Time in Sweet Silence

*Come away, my beloved,* God whispers to you. He calls you to go to a quiet place, to still your soul, and to let the silence speak to you. Hushing your busy thoughts and taking a break from the business of life helps you gain clearer insight on what is happening into your life.

silence

One of the gifts of living more simply is having more time for silence, prayer, and contemplation. When you spend time in sweet silence, you disconnect from the flurry of daily life and enter an eternal, God-centered perspective. Allow the silence to teach you the gentle rhythms of grace.

> *The LORD your God is with you, he is mighty to save. He will take great delight in you, he will quiet you with his love, he will rejoice over you with singing.*
>
> Zephaniah 3:17 NIV

≫ Take time out for communing with the Lord in silence. Go out in nature and let the birds sing you a love song from God.

# #38
## Look for Hidden Possibilities

*Great opportunities come to all, but many do not know they have met them. The only preparation to take advantage of them is simple fidelity to watch what each day brings.*

Albert E. Dunning

look

Practical, simple wisdom teaches you to look for the hidden possibilities in places or things that others overlook. Most people see briars and brambles beside the path, but you discover the ripe blackberries that will make a delicious pie. The racks at the Goodwill store hold designer duds for pennies if you know what to look for.

Seek out the hidden possibilities in people, too. An awkward adolescent hides beautiful dreams in her heart. The old man next door may hide a heart of gold under his gruff exterior. You can discover possibilities everywhere, if you have the eyes to see.

≫ Look for the hidden possibilities in the life you lead today by paying attention to what others ignore or pass by.

# #39

## Take Time for a Picnic

Don't bother to set the table. Make a sandwich or toss a salad instead of cooking. Add some fruit and cookies, along with something to drink. Then take your favorite picnic basket (or brown bag) outdoors to enjoy an impromptu picnic in your backyard or at a local park. It's an easy break from the usual routine.

Getting outside will lift your spirits. If you work in an office, taking a lunch break outdoors gives your soul a rest from the business atmosphere. Remember that his eye is on the sparrow, so feed the birds some breadcrumbs too.

picnic

*I love to think of nature as an unlimited broadcasting station, through which God speaks to us every hour, if we will only tune in.*

George Washington Carver

>> Be prepared for impromptu picnics by investing in a simple picnic basket and stocking it with picnic supplies (napkins, cups, paper plates, plasticware).

# #40

## Enjoy the Company of Others

*May the Lord make you increase and abound in love to one another and to all, just as we do to you.*

1 Thessalonians 3:12
NKJV

others

One of the rewards of simplifying your life is that you have more time for friends and family. Being with loved ones can energize and encourage you, especially if you don't have to rush to the next appointment or squeeze in one more thing on your to-do list.

Sit back. Relax. Enjoy being with others and revel in these precious moments spent with the people God has placed in your life. These relationships are more important than any outward accomplishment will ever be. So make the time and create the occasions for everyone to get together and enjoy one another's company.

≫ Strengthen your connection with friends and loved ones by praying for each person by name on a regular basis.

# #41

## Invest in Education

Widen your horizons and commit to lifelong learning. Education is a great value that pays dividends long after class is over. You'll be richer in understanding for every hour invested.

Challenging yourself with classes or workshops keeps you from being stuck in a rut. Education can help you make better choices as you work on creating a simpler and more effective life. At the very least, you'll have a good time learning something new and meeting new people. Look for ways to enhance your spiritual life through education too. Join a Bible-study group, attend a workshop on personal growth, or read a spiritual book.

*invest*

*Wise men and women are always learning, always listening for fresh insights.*

Proverbs 18:15 MSG

>> Investigate educational offerings in your area: community colleges, special courses, private lessons. Choose something that you think would be fun to take.

# #42

## Love Your Work

*In the noise and clatter of my kitchen . . . I possess God in great tranquility as if I were upon my knees.*

Brother Lawrence

work

It takes more energy to resist and complain than it does to have a positive attitude. Whether you like your job or wish you could be anywhere else, choosing to love your work can create a positive transformation in the way your workday unfolds.

If you are doing a mundane task, offer it to God and give it your best effort. Use it as a form of prayer or meditation. If the task is exciting and creative, ask God to show you how to do it even better. Turn work into a love offering, appreciating the gifts that come with earning your daily bread.

≫ Ask God to help you see the blessings in your job: companionship, money earned, useful work accomplished, another step toward a cherished goal.

# #43

## Practice Patience

Green apples need a time of ripening before they become fully red and ready to eat. You can pick them early, but all you'll end up with is a sour taste and an upset stomach. Be patient and wait until the fruit is ripe. It's easier in the long run to wait until the timing is right, whether with fruit or with the circumstances of your life.

Make it easier on yourself by practicing patience and waiting on God's perfect timing. Patience is not passivity. It is an opportunity to partner with God. Let your heart be quiet and trust in divine timing.

patience

> *Think of farmers who wait patiently for the spring and summer rains to make their valuable crops grow. Be patient like those farmers and don't give up.*
>
> James 5:7–8 CEV

>> When you are stuck in traffic or waiting in line, use the wait to connect with God and become calm and quiet in his presence.

# #44

## Get Plenty of Rest

*Sleep re-creates.
The Bible indicates
that sleep is not
meant only for the
recuperation of a
man's body, but that
there is a tremendous
furtherance of spiri-
tual and moral life
during sleep.*

Oswald Chambers

rest

Getting more sleep is a simple solution for reducing stress and making things easier on yourself. If you've been trying to do more than you can comfortably handle, cut back on some of your activities and honor your body's need for rest. Make getting enough rest a priority and you will be rewarded with energy, clear thinking, and a relaxed attitude toward the ups and downs of life.

You'll be happier when you're rested, and you'll make wiser decisions. You'll be less likely to make mistakes or overlook important details and instead be more alert to what God is doing in your life.

>> Make yourself go to bed at least one hour early tonight. You'll find the extra rest will help you wake up more refreshed in the morning.

# #45

## Let Go of Grudges

Holding on to anger and grudges steals energy from your life. Every time you complain, to others or to yourself, about what someone has done or left undone, you make the wrong worse. No matter what the other person has done, letting go of grudges makes life simpler for you.

Ask God to help you forgive others as he has forgiven you. Choose to focus on more positive thoughts by being thankful for what's right in your life instead of rerunning old wrongs in your mind. You'll find you have more energy to enjoy life because your own negativity is no longer draining you.

forgive

> *Be kind and merciful, and forgive others, just as God forgave you because of Christ.*
>
> Ephesians 4:32 CEV

>> If you have been complaining about a wrong someone did to you, stop. Instead of dwelling on it, choose to forgive that person and move on.

# #46
## Tell Your Truth

> *Truth is not only violated by falsehood; it may be equally outraged by silence.*
>
> Henri-Frédéric Amiel

truth

Remember the peer pressures of adolescence? Some teens would do anything to fit in with the crowd. Even as an adult, it's a game that's all too easy to play. What a relief it is to take off the mask of conformity and admit who you really are inside.

Make your life simpler by choosing authenticity over conformity. Trust your heart's wisdom and be brave enough to stand up for what you believe. Instead of working so hard to be who you think others want you to be, relax and be yourself. God will honor your honesty, and you'll feel better about yourself.

≫ Start with an inner truth inventory: have you been avoiding a truth you don't want to admit to yourself? Ask God to give you wisdom on this issue.

# #47

## Make It Yourself

The do-it-yourself philosophy is the essence of simple living. You might knit a scarf or sweater to warm you in winter, or build a bookshelf to fit perfectly in a corner in your office, or bake a chocolate cake from scratch to satisfy your creativity. Making something offers personal rewards that are priceless. A handmade, homemade object has its own beauty, as well as the satisfaction you receive from creating something with your own skills and ingenuity.

Working with your hands gives you time to meditate on your life and nurture your spirit. Enjoy the simple pleasure of creating something with your own two hands.

make

> *There are few things as effective in bringing us back to ourselves and to our connection to life and creativity as doing something with our own hands.*
>
> Alexandra Stoddard

>> Take a crafts or arts class and have fun creating handmade gifts for others or useful and beautiful objects for your own enjoyment.

stretch

# 101 ways to

rejoice

beautify

renew

hush

# simplify your life

seek

relax

enhance

# #48

## Clean House

> *An hour's industry
> will do more to
> produce cheerfulness,
> suppress evil humors,
> and retrieve your
> affairs than a
> month's moaning.*
>
> Benjamin Franklin

## clean

Cleaning house is like cleansing and ordering your life. You can ignore mess, but it is still a distraction, like a squeaky wheel or a dripping faucet. Conquer dust and sticky floors with a mop, broom, and duster, and create an oasis of restful cleanliness and order in your home. Things run more smoothly when the house is freshly cleaned and the atmosphere is lightened by your elbow grease.

Use your housecleaning time to put your thoughts in order, too. There is something about repetitive work that allows the mind to think more clearly, and cleaning house can be symbolic of other cleansing and ordering in your life.

>> If you don't have time to do a thorough housecleaning, concentrate on one room and get it cleaned and in order.

# #49

## Reserve Judgment

Snap decisions can complicate life. Being too quick to state your opinion could put you in an uncomfortable corner. There are plenty of so-called experts who will offer an opinion on what someone has done or what will happen tomorrow, but there are few wise souls who are willing to suspend judgment to wait and see what unfolds.

When others are quick to judge or predict outcomes, keep quiet. People with easy answers often don't even know what the real question is. Quiet prudence can keep you focused on what's truly important. Allow God to be your guide, and leave the judging up to him.

reserve

*Do you see a man who speaks in haste? There is more hope for a fool than for him.*

Proverbs 29:20 NIV

>> Take time to weigh the facts in any situation. Give yourself time to quietly assess what is happening before you state an opinion or make a commitment.

# #50
## Take Off Your Shoes

*Lord, purge our eyes to see within the seed a tree, within the glowing egg a bird, within the shroud a butterfly, till, taught by such, we see beyond all creatures, thee.*

Christina Rossetti

shoes

When Moses saw the burning bush in the desert, he was curious and went to see this unusual sight. Then he heard a voice from within the bush commanding him to take off his shoes, for he was standing on holy ground. He realized that God was speaking to him.

Nature speaks of the greatness of the Creator. Decide today that you will take off your shoes and wiggle your toes in the grass, allowing a childlike spirit to speak to your heart. You can find God's glory in any suburban yard, for even a common green lawn will shout his praise.

≫ Go barefoot in the grass and take the time to enjoy small things like butterflies and flowers and earthworms, seeing God's creative hand in them.

# #51

## Feed the Birds

The hummingbird's wings move like a living helicopter as it hovers over the red birdfeeder. Shy sparrows and sassy blue jays compete for the seeds you toss out on the snow. Winged messengers speak of God's glory, reminding you that his eye is on the sparrow.

birds

The simple pleasure of feeding the birds creates a moment of wonder in the day. You can spread a feast for fine feathered friends in your backyard, whether you have elaborate birdhouses and feeders or whether you just sprinkle some birdseed on the lawn. Or you can take bread to feed ducks and enjoy the show at a local lake.

> *Even the sparrow has found a home, and the swallow a nest for herself, where she may have her young.*
>
> Psalm 84:3 NIV

≫ Set up a birdfeeder and birdbath in your backyard. Enjoy the seasonal show as birds of a feather feed together.

# #52

## Create Simple Entertainment

*Have fun at your party and embrace the unexpected. Celebrate your family, friends, and food! Laugh, sing, dance, and eat.*

Tamara Weiss

simple

Feeding the birds offers one simple form of entertainment. Inexpensive homemade entertainment can also include old-fashioned games like charades or musical chairs. Tossing a Frisbee in the park, playing tag, or setting up a game of volleyball brings people together to enjoy their own amusements.

Have a movie evening with plenty of popcorn to share with friends or family. Host a simple potluck to celebrate a full moon or the first rose of summer or the last day before school starts. The simplest things can bring friends and family together for a good time.

>> Gather a few friends for an easy potluck picnic in the park. Bring a Frisbee or a ball and enjoy a game of catch before sitting down to eat.

# #53

## Clean a Closet

Life is much easier when your living space is clear of clutter. You are able to find what you need without scrabbling through piles of miscellaneous junk. An ordered space in which to live and work seems to give you more mental space for creative thinking. You will breathe a sigh of relief in the pristine order and beauty you have created.

closet

The mountain of cleaning and clearing may look daunting, but take it one small step at a time. Start with a closet or cupboard to put in order. Then you'll have the pleasant accomplishment of one cleared space to encourage your further efforts. *even a drawer!*

> *Slack habits and sloppy work are as bad as vandalism.*
> Proverbs 18:9 MSG

≫ If you can't vacuum, sweep, dust, and mop everything in one day, tackle one or two rooms, and just straighten and fluff in the rest of the house.

# #54

## Create a Barter Network

> *A thing is worth precisely what it can do for you; not what you choose to pay for it.*
>
> John Ruskin

barter

Your friend is super with plumbing, and you've got a stopped-up toilet. He loves your apple pie, so trade your pie for his plumbing service. You're a whiz at computers, and your computer-phobic buddy has a software problem. You'd love to have her help at next week's yard sale, so you strike a deal that pleases both parties.

You don't always have to pay full price for goods and services. Consider the art of the trade, and pool your resources to help one another out. A barter network could save you money and simplify your life—and create a network of friendly support for all concerned.

>> Brainstorm with your friends and create a list of friends with skills and a list of friends with needs. See how you can match them up creatively.

# #55

## Exercise to Lift Your Spirits

Enjoy the simple lift that exercise offers. God gave you a body that likes to be in motion, and there is exhilaration in traveling down a road with your own two feet, swinging your arms, and feeling the wind in your face.

Exercise gives you a much-needed break from sedentary activities. You feel more invigorated, think more clearly, and have greater zest for life. Exercise can also offer a simple way to meditate. As you get into the rhythm of movement, it clears your mind and helps you focus your thoughts.

exercise

*Walking requires little in the way of equipment or planning or physical conditioning, but it gives you the world.*

Ann H. Zwinger

>> Try to get out and walk twenty minutes every other day. Check out exercise options at your local YMCA or exercise club.

# #56

## Enjoy the Weather

*Praise the LORD from the earth, you great sea creatures and all ocean depths, lightning and hail, snow and clouds, stormy winds that do his bidding.*

Psalm 148:7–8 NIV

weather

You can't change the weather, so you might as well enjoy it. The essence of simple living is to enjoy what comes and accept what is. If it's a bright, sun-shiny day, have a picnic. If the clouds are pouring down liquid sunshine, get out your umbrella and waterproof boots and walk in the rain.

Enjoying the weather outdoors as it comes reminds you to accept the weather of your interior life, too. Some days will be sad and low-key. Just give them to God and do your best. Other days will have a sunnier outlook. Praise God and make the most of them.

≫ Go out for a walk with a friend. You'll enjoy good conversation as well as the exhilaration of moving your body in the great outdoors.

# #57

## Cook Nourishing Meals

Honor the body God has given you. Take care of yourself and avoid unnecessary illness by eating well. Nourishing meals help you stay healthy and fit. Fast food won't make you feel taken care of and nurtured like a home-cooked meal will.

For instance, cook a hearty stew in the slow cooker. It can simmer while you're away all day. When you get home, toss a green salad, add some bread and fruit, and you have a satisfying meal. Save the leftovers for another day. It's a simple solution for you to eat well and to take good care of yourself.

cook

*You let the earth produce grass for cattle, plants for our food, wine to cheer us up, olive oil for our skin, and grain for our health.*

Psalm 104:14–15
CEV

>> Invest in a slow cooker and make hearty, slow-cooked meals that will be ready to eat when you come home at night.

# #58

## Clear Your Schedule for a Day

*I learned the interior of life was as rich as the exterior life, and that my richest moments occurred when I was absolutely still.*

Richard Bode

schedule

When you're healthy and able to keep your commitments, having a whole day for yourself seems like an impossible extravagance. Yet if you became sick and unable to meet your obligations, you would have no choice but to clear your schedule. Taking a day off is a prescription for keeping priorities straight and celebrating the simple joys of life.

Give yourself the gift of one whole day off to rest, recuperate, and tend to your soul. Nurturing your inner life helps you order your outer life and restores your energy. Consider this day away as an utterly necessary appointment with God, a time to become still in his presence.

≫ If you have family obligations and need help, trade childcare or home help with a friend, and give him or her a much-needed day off too.

# #59

## Harvest Happiness

Gifts of happiness are waiting for you, if you are willing to look for them. God scatters the seeds of life's little wonders, pleasures, and joys throughout your day. Small gifts like fresh flowers, hugs, sunshine, birdsong, and friends and family who love you offer the kind of happiness that grows from contentment.

This kind of happiness does not depend on big events or monumental achievements. It comes from the daily blessings that are often taken for granted. If you have food, shelter, and good work to do, you are rich. Harvest happiness from daily living and enjoy life's simple blessings.

harvest

> *Happiness is not a possession to be prized, it is a quality of thought, a state of mind.*
>
> Daphne du Maurier

>> Appreciate the little blessings of daily life. Think about how you can multiply the harvest of happiness by sharing these simple gifts with others.

# #60

## Do What Needs Doing Now

> *If you know the right thing to do and don't do it, that, for you, is evil.*
>
> James 4:17 MSG

do

You have the best of intentions, but when life is full and busy, it's easy to procrastinate and let unpleasant tasks slide. Tackle neglected tasks now and clear clutter to simplify your life. Choose to overcome procrastination by setting small, measurable goals—then follow through on them.

When you get your car serviced, mark the projected date for the next oil change on your calendar. Open and sort your mail the day you receive it. Take action on a small task, such as returning a phone call, right away instead of putting it off until tomorrow.

>> Partner with a friend as you both challenge habits of procrastination. Support each other by setting small, measurable goals for simplifying life.

# #61

## Count Each Moment as Holy

The river of time flows swiftly by. The circle of seasons goes round, each with its own special flavor. Good times with friends and family soon become sweet memories. Looking back at what has been, you realize that the fleeting moments are precious.

Counting each moment as holy brings focus and clarity to what's most important to you right now. Live as if each moment is a gift from God. When you pay attention to what's happening in the here and now, you create an oasis of eternity with your appreciation. You can't stop time, but you can expand it by fully appreciating the present time.

holy

*Take care of the minutes, for the hours will take care of themselves.*

Lord Chesterfield

≫ The next time you enjoy a meal with family or friends, look around the table at each loved one and savor the moment as well as the food.

# #62

## Practice Moderation

> *Let your*
> *gentleness*
> *be known to*
> *everyone. The*
> *Lord is near.*
>
> Philippians 4:5 NRSV

practice

When was the last time you went to a potluck and practiced moderation? With all those tempting dishes, it probably was easy to pile the food too high on the plate. Well, in some ways, life is like a potluck—and it's hard not to overdo.

Moderation as a godly virtue sounds boring, but life is simpler and easier when you take only what you need and no more. Instead of an upset stomach from overeating, savor a few flavors and feel satisfied. Spend less instead of piling up credit-card debt. Cut back on your schedule when you are feeling overwhelmed.

>> Practice moderation when you start a new exercise plan. Take it in slow, easy steps instead of wearing yourself out on the first day.

# #63

## Pay Off Your Debts

debts

Reduce stress—and interest payments. If you have a balance on your credit cards, look for ways to pay it off as soon as possible. Owing money, especially on high-interest credit cards, steals energy from you. It's more difficult to make the right choices for your life if you are worried about how you're going to make your monthly credit payments.

Paying off your debts offers more dividends than just money. Debt becomes a burden you no longer have to carry. A debt-free life is easier and offers more choices. A debt-free life enables you to plan and budget your money for more important things.

> *Don't be obsessed with getting more material things. Be relaxed with what you have. . . . God assured us, "I'll never let you down, never walk off and leave you."*
>
> Hebrews 13:5 MSG

≫ Draw up a budget for paying off your debts. Consider creative alternatives such as selling something to help you get free of debt sooner.

clean

101 ways to

allow

decide

play

meditate

# simplify your life

barter

exercise

walk

# #64

## Admit Your Errors

*One of the hardest things in the world to do is to admit you are wrong. And nothing is more helpful in resolving a situation than its frank admission.*

Benjamin Disraeli

errors

It takes a humble heart to admit that you made a mistake. If you are challenged, your first reaction might be to defend and explain your position, or even deny that there is a problem. But it's easier and simpler to admit mistakes than to keep resisting a difficult truth.

Others will usually forgive an honest error and admire the person who is willing to admit to making a mistake. Be willing to admit your errors, look for ways to improve, and move on. Trust that God will honor your honesty and willingness to let go of pride. You'll save time and energy when you do.

≫ The next time you find yourself opening your mouth to defend a decision you made, be still. Trust God that he will reveal the truth of the situation.

# #65

## Enjoy Good Conversation

Laughing and talking with good friends energizes you. When the conversation is flowing and everyone makes a witty or wise contribution, people feel good. Celebrate the fact that by simplifying your life you've created room for more good times with friends.

Make a positive contribution to the conversation. When negative comments or inappropriate language surfaces, turn the conversation to more uplifting topics. Avoid hurting anyone's feelings. Say nothing that you would be ashamed to say if you were speaking to God. Make life easier for yourself and others by encouraging the positive over the negative in conversation.

enjoy

> *Watch the way you talk. Let nothing foul or dirty come out of your mouth. Say only what helps, each word a gift.*
>
> Ephesians 4:29 MSG

≫ Say nothing the next time you are tempted to complain or criticize. Talk only when you can offer something helpful or positive to the conversation.

# #66

## Laugh at Your Mistakes

*The man who makes no mistakes lacks boldness and the spirit of adventure. He never tries anything new. He is a brake on the wheels of progress.*

M. W. Larmour

laugh

Taking yourself more lightly greases the wheels of life. Instead of carrying a burden of self-importance and the need to justify every choice, you are free to make mistakes as well as to try new things. Realize that you win some and you lose some. Laughing at mistakes allows you to view mistakes as opportunities to learn and grow instead of as disasters to deny or defend.

Life is a process of learning. God knows your heart and knows that mistakes are part of the process. Forgive yourself as God forgives you. Like a child who stumbles as she's learning to walk, pick yourself up and keep on walking.

≫ Stretch yourself by trying a new and fun activity, and when you make mistakes, see them as part of the learning process instead of as failures.

# #67

## Keep Paper in Its Place

Does it sometimes feel like a blizzard has landed on your desk? If you are constantly digging through papers to find what you need, organizing your papers and creating a filing system can make work simpler and less time-consuming.

Start by sorting papers in order of importance. Invest in filing systems or organizers that help you tame your papers. Have a place for everything, and keep up with your to-be-filed box. Be ruthless in eliminating papers you no longer need. When you keep paper in its place, you have control over it instead of its having control over you.

paper

> *Once mastered, you will consider organizing to be an incredibly cleansing and empowering process—an exhilarating way of freeing yourself up and maintaining a steady life course in a complex world.*
>
> Julie Morgenstern

≫ Set aside a box or basket for newspapers to recycle. Donate old magazines to medical offices or nursing homes.

# #68

## Listen to Your Body

*There is a spirit in man, and the breath of the Almighty gives him understanding.*

Job 32:8 NKJV

listen

Your body has a God-given wisdom all its own. Take advantage of this built-in guidance system and listen to your body when it tells you something. Paying attention to your gut feelings and to the signals your body sends can offer inner guidance that simplifies the deci-sion-making process.

Your body speaks to you through feelings of uneasiness when a situation is dangerous. A gut-wrenching stomach twist or a feeling of physical heaviness may warn you of trouble or danger. As you weigh the pros and cons of a choice, bring body, mind, and spirit into the decision process.

≫ The next time you are feeling tired, instead of pushing yourself harder, take time to rest.

# #69

## Converse Continually with God

Hourly prayer is a simple way to sustain the connection of grace as you go through the day. You don't need alarms or rigid rituals—just the awareness that God is always there to listen if you wish to converse with him.

Choose to be like the child who knows that God is intimately interested in all that he or she has to say and in everything that happens, no matter how small or trivial it might seem to others. Practice prayer as a relationship that's as essential and simple as daily bread. Listen for God's guidance; it will help you sort and clarify priorities.

converse

*There is not in the world a kind of life more sweet and delightful than that of a continual conversation with God.*

Brother Lawrence

>> Prayer is talking with God. Use a small reminder, such as a phone ringing or a bird singing, to prompt a moment's prayed conversation in your day.

# #70

## Change Your Inner Dialogue

*God wants us to love ourselves with His love. He wants us to think His thoughts about ourselves — thoughts of kindness, esteem, respect, and trust.*

Floyd McClung Jr.

change

The voice of your inner critic concentrates on what's wrong. When you listen to your inner critic's sneering voice, nothing you do or say is ever good enough. Such negative inner dialogue keeps you from doing your best or trying something new. Change your inner dialogue by seeing yourself through God's eyes.

In God's eyes you are a beloved child. Just as a parent would not chastise a child for falling down who is just learning to walk, so God encourages you to get up when you fall down and to keep going. Make it easier on yourself by replacing disparaging negativity with encouraging, life-affirming thoughts.

≫ When critical or negative thoughts arise, replace them with the truth of God's love, acceptance, and grace.

# #71

## Buy Fresh and in Season

A tender ear of fresh corn has a sweetness that no canned or frozen corn can duplicate. Those luscious, ripe, red tomatoes of late summer are at their highest peak of flavor and the lowest prices of the year. Whether it's the first spring asparagus or the last fall pumpkin, buying food fresh and in season will give you the greatest flavor and variety for the best price.

Buying in season makes meal planning simpler. Enjoy the foods of each season and create the dishes that take advantage of natural patterns of fruitfulness and flavor. Thank God for the harvest bounty.

fresh

*The LORD your God will bless you in all your harvest and in all the work of your hands, and your joy will be complete.*

Deuteronomy 16:15
NIV

>> Go to a local farmers' market and enjoy the display of fresh produce. Buy some fresh fruits and veggies to take home for a simple, seasonal meal.

# #72
## Do What Makes Your Heart Sing

> *Everyone should carefully observe which way his heart draws him, and then choose that way with all his strength.*
>
> Jewish Proverb

sing

You have more energy and joy when you do what makes your heart sing. You go through life with ease and grace instead of struggling with frustration when you invest your energy in what you love. Your choice of what to do or what not to do becomes simple and clear when you discover something that makes your heart sing.

This heartfelt way of living is worlds apart from dry drudgery or frantic fearfulness. A musician loves the music, an athlete loves the sport, a teacher loves the learning. When you let love lead the way, you allow God's grace to support your endeavors.

>> Give yourself permission to enjoy a better-quality life by investing time and energy in something you love.

# #73

## Learn the Wisdom of Play

Child's play creates new options and brings lively energy into your life. Serious workaholics are especially in need of the creative therapy of child's play. Having a good time is good for the soul, and it helps you gain much-needed perspective on what's truly important in life.

It doesn't take a lot of time or expense to learn the wisdom of play. A great adult escape might be taking time out for a game of catch, puttering around in the kitchen trying a new recipe, or enjoying an hour in the shop working with wood. A playful spirit expresses the joy of the Lord.

play

*Jesus answered and said, "I thank You, Father, Lord of heaven and earth, that You have hidden these things from the wise and prudent and have revealed them to babes."*

Matthew 11:25
NKJV

>> Spend time with children or watching children play. Notice how naturally and easily they embrace each experience and learn as they have fun.

# #74

## Relax in God's Timing

*I trust in you,
O LORD; I say,
"You are my God."
My times are in
your hands.*

Psalm 31:14–15 NIV

relax

God's timing is perfect. Life becomes much simpler when you learn to trust his timetable instead of fretting that your life is not moving ahead according to schedule. Relax into the rhythm of life as it is, even when you'd like it to move slower or faster.

Savor each moment and trust God. Then you can relax and enjoy your life instead of wishing it away or wasting time worrying. Appreciate today's blessings and know that God will provide what you need when you need it. Believe that God holds past, present, and future in his hands, and rest in his loving care.

≫ Get up a bit earlier tomorrow morning to give yourself some extra time to start the day with God.

# #75

## Create Goals with Heart

There are many worthy goals you can accomplish. But just because a goal is worthy does not mean that it's a goal you should aim for. God created you with unique gifts and a particular temperament and set of interests. When you throw your whole heart into something that you love, you do it better and enjoy it more.

Give yourself permission to follow your heart. If you create goals that reflect your heart's priorities, you'll discover a simpler and more fulfilling way to approach life. When love motivates you, it reflects the same kind of love God had when he created the world.

goals

*No one can be making much of his life who has not a very definite conception of what he is living for.*

Henry Drummond

>> Evaluate your present goals in light of what you love. Set a goal that lifts your heart with anticipation, and watch how easily you accomplish it.

# #76

## Never Give Up

> *Those who hope in the LORD will renew their strength. They will soar on wings like eagles; they will run and not grow weary, they will walk and not be faint.*
>
> Isaiah 40:31 NIV

never

Choosing to simplify your life is an act of hope and courage. No matter how complex modern life may be or how knotty the problems are that must be untangled, you can trust God to help you change your life for the better. He is the foundation of your hope and strength.

Never give up, even when you are most discouraged. Trust that you are not alone. Nurture the hope within you by turning to God and asking him to be your strength. Believe that he will lead you, one step at a time, into greater clarity and simplicity and joy.

≫ Spend time with hopeful and encouraging people. Encourage others in their hopes and dreams.

# #77

## Accept Your Limitations

When you were young, anything seemed possible; any goal seemed reachable. But life goes on, choices are made, and you grow older and wiser. You learn that you are finite and that only God has infinite power. Being the person God created you to be comes through accepting your weaknesses as well as developing your strengths.

Accepting the limitations of human life can be an act of trust in a gracious God. Instead of resisting and rebelling, make life simpler by accepting what is and working with that. Your acceptance frees you to trust in the God who can transcend your limitations.

accept

> *Jesus looked at them and said, "There are some things that people cannot do, but God can do anything."*
>
> Mark 10:27 CEV

>> Keep a childhood dream alive in adulthood by exploring that interest. You may never be an astronaut, but you can always gaze at the stars.

# #78

## Make the Best of It

*A cheerful disposition is good for your health; gloom and doom leave you bone-tired.*

Proverbs 17:22 MSG

best

No matter what your circumstances may be, a simple change of attitude can make them better. Making the best of a situation helps you cope with difficulties and make more of opportunities. Like a great sailing ship setting its sails to take advantage of the wind whichever direction it may blow, your life is moved in positive directions by choosing to make the best of whatever comes.

Look for ways to turn a less than perfect situation into the right situation for you. Instead of complaining, ask God to show you how to make things better. Do your best. Trust God with the rest.

≫ The next time you are standing in line at the grocery store or you are waiting for a delayed flight, look for ways you can make the best of the situation.

# #79

## Enjoy Frugal Extravagances

It doesn't take much to make life feel abundant and rich. Simple things like a pair of new socks, a bouquet of fresh flowers, or a season ticket in the bleachers can make the simple life feel extravagantly luxurious with little outlay of cash.

Enjoy frugal extravagances such as a pint of fresh raspberries for dessert or a subscription to one of your favorite magazines. Small but simple pleasures make you feel cared for. Taking delight in little luxuries keeps you from feeling deprived. Then you'll be less inclined to exceed your budget or binge on expensive or wasteful extravagances.

frugal

> *Be ready at all times for the gifts of God, and always for new ones.*
>
> Meister Eckhart

>> Indulge in the frugal extravagance of time to do something you want or to do nothing. Enjoy extra quiet time in God's presence or with loved ones.

admit

# 101 ways to

laugh

talk

stretch

sort

# simplify your life

listen

pray

change

# #80

## Leave Yesterday in the Past

*There is no past we can bring back by longing for it. There is only an eternal now that builds and creates out of the past something new and better.*

Johann Wolfgang von Goethe

past

When you leave yesterday in the past and trust God with the future, you simplify life here and now. You are free to focus on what is, and to embrace and enjoy the gifts God wants to lavish on you in this time and place.

Appreciate the present moment as a gift from God. Focusing on the moment brings you into God's presence. While you might have regrets about what you left undone, or you might miss what you left behind, the only moment you have is right now. It is an act of praise and faith to fully embrace life in this moment.

≫ Be present and at ease in this moment. Be aware of what you sense—sight, sound, scent, touch, and taste—and fully experience the here and now.

# #81

## Enjoy a Childhood Pleasure

Remember the pleasures of childhood? Swings. Sandlot baseball. The smell of crayons and the satisfaction of filling a page with color. Finger painting and modeling clay and papier-mâché. Romps in the grass. The cool treat of an ice-cream cone. A cozy corner with a favorite book.

Renew your sense of youth and adventure and fun. Reconnect with what you loved as a child. Indulge in a favorite dessert. Buy crayons and a coloring book and color to your heart's delight. Letting go of grown-up complexities and enjoying simple childhood pleasures remind you of essentials of the heart and infuse adulthood with creative joy.

enjoy

*A world without children is a world without newness, regeneration, color, and vigor.*

James Dobson

>> Take a trip to a zoo, a county fair, or an amusement park. Indulge in a special childhood food: popcorn, cotton candy, or ice cream.

# #82

## Give Your Worries to God

*Strive first for the kingdom of God and his righteousness, and all these things will be given to you as well.*

Matthew 6:33 NRSV

give

Worry is a thief. It steals your energy and attention but solves nothing. Simple faith will help you deal with complex problems. When you are worried, exchange anxious thinking for faith-based affirmation. Focus on the power and greatness of your loving God, who is larger than any problem or fear you may face. Speak affirming words of trust and faith, and give your worries to God.

Choose an affirmative phrase such as "God is my strength" on which to meditate. Having an active trust in the power of God will free you from worry and enable you to make life an adventure, instead of an obstacle course.

≫ Break away from worrisome thoughts by involving your body as well as your mind: light a candle, read Scripture, sing praises, and pray aloud.

# #83

## Keep It Simple, Sweetheart

It seems obvious to say tell you to keep it simple. But how often have you found yourself tangled in red tape and self-created chaos because you made a simple thing more complex than it had to be? Making life changes needn't be a big production. Focus on essentials and take short, easy steps.

Be kind to yourself. No need to end those family words with the popular *stupid*. Be gentle with yourself and say *sweetheart,* "Keep it simple, sweetheart." You are beloved by God, so let your words and attitudes reflect that fact. Reward yourself when you do well, forgive yourself when you fall down. Take simple steps and walk in the light of love.

s i m p l e

> *Making the simple complicated is commonplace; making the complicated simple, awesomely simple, that's creativity.*
>
> Charles Mingus

>> The next time you reach a goal, applaud and reward yourself before you plunge into the next goal. Take time to savor your accomplishment.

# #84
## Make Friends Your Allies

> *Everyone helped his neighbor, and said to his brother, "Be of good courage!"*
>
> Isaiah 41:6 NKJV

allies

Friends can be your greatest allies in the quest for a simpler and more meaningful way of life. They can encourage you when you're weary and remind you to stick to your goals when you are tempted to stray. Spend time with encouraging friends who share the same goals and values. Give less energy to relationships that drain or distract you.

You can partner with a friend and hold each other accountable as you work together to create a simpler lifestyle. Get together on a regular basis and compare notes. Brainstorm creative ideas for each other, and lend a helping hand when you can.

≫ Call a trusted friend this week and get together to brainstorm ideas on how to live more simply. Take one idea and apply it, and then compare notes on what happened.

# #85

## Create a Plan

A plan helps you to simplify your life. You create a plan of action, and God helps you see it through. Planning helps you focus your efforts and energies and offers a way to measure what you've done and how far you've come. Whether you plan a day or a month, a good plan keeps you focused on your purposes and goals.

Make manageable plans. Grandiose schemes are counterproductive. Simple action steps that are easily measurable will help you keep going when the going gets tough. Include room in your plans for the unexpected. Leave space for grace to bring delightful surprises.

plan

*Planning is bringing the future into the present so you can do something about it now.*

Alan Lakein

>> Review the things you value in life. Make a monthly plan to bring more balance, serenity, and simplicity into your life.

# #86

## Live Under Your Means

> *Get all you can, save all you can, and give all you can.*
>
> John Wesley

means

Instead of spending every penny you earn, cut back on expenses and live under your means. Set a portion of your money aside for savings and for giving and tithes. You'll breathe a sigh of relief knowing that you have some money socked away and that there is more room and flexibility in your budget. Make money your servant.

Watch for small expenses that can add up quickly. If you cut out that three-dollar daily latte for the five-day work-week, you'll save fifteen dollars. Life is easier and simpler with some financial breathing space. Lowering expenses can make you feel as though you're getting a raise in pay.

≫ Keep track of your daily expenses for a week. Look at your spending patterns, and decide where you need to cut back.

# #87

## Pay Bills Promptly

Forget past-due notices, late fees, and the hassle of trying to find out if a check went through on time. Make life simpler by paying bills promptly and on time. Honor your obligations and take care of business. If you appreciate prompt payment when others owe you, do the same when you owe others. Your creditors will appreciate it.

Paying what you owe promptly is a statement of faith in God's ability to provide for your needs. It also makes keeping track of expenses easier. You will have peace of mind when you know that you have met every obligation and have done your part to keep things straight between you and the ones you owe.

*bills*

*God is able to make all grace abound toward you, that you, always having all sufficiency in all things, may have an abundance for every good work.*

2 Corinthians 9:8
NKJV

≫ As an act of faith in God's abundant supply, tithe a portion of your income first. Start with 10 percent and plan to grow in your giving.

# #88

## Take a Home Retreat

*He is happiest, be he king or peasant, who finds peace in his home.*

Johann Wolfgang von Goethe

retreat

Take a home retreat and pamper yourself as a simple way to deal with stress. You may not be able to stay at a bed-and-breakfast or relax at an expensive spa, but you can create a home retreat that will allow you time and space for rest, relaxation, and renewal, without the expense of travel or the bother of packing a suitcase.

Sleep in and enjoy the comfort of your own bed. Cuddle under the covers and revel in a morning without deadlines or to-do lists. Take a leisurely bath. Unplug the phone, turn off the computer, and let your soul soak in the silence.

≫ Take a break from self-improvement or required reading and curl up with an engrossing novel.

# #89
## Make Incremental Changes

Giant leaps can be scary. But baby steps are doable. Small, incremental changes are less intimidating and will take you over the long haul. Life is less complicated when you don't attempt to do more than you can easily do.

Whether you are getting in shape, contemplating a career change, or clearing clutter from your office, small and easy actions will add up to big changes over time. Start slowly and build gently. Most growth, including spiritual growth, comes gradually and often imperceptibly. You may not realize how far you've come or how much you've accomplished until you look back over time.

changes

> *Commit your way to the LORD, trust also in Him, and He shall bring it to pass.*
>
> Psalm 37:5 NKJV

>> Think about a goal you want to accomplish. List the steps you need to take, and break each step into simple, small-action steps.

# #90

## Transform Your Relationship to Money

> *If a person gets his attitude toward money straight, it will help straighten out almost every other area in his life.*
>
> Billy Graham

transform

Simplify complex financial matters by transforming your relationship to money. Instead of allowing money to control you, learn to see it as a force you can control. Respect money instead of fearing it. Educate yourself about money matters: debt and interest, savings, investing, budgets, spreadsheets, taxes, and so forth. You'll make better decisions when you understand how money works.

Part of choosing a simple lifestyle is learning to make better decisions concerning money. Wise use of God-given resources, including money, can help you create a more fulfilling and satisfying life.

≫ *Financial Peace* by Dave Ramsey covers financial basics and shows how to make money work for you instead of your working for money.

# #91

## Acquire Experiences Instead of Things

Creating a simpler life makes you weigh your values. Things can be wonderful, but they break, wear out, and clutter your home. Life is precious and fleeting, so value life and feed your spirit by putting material things second. Invest in life experiences such as education and self-improvement, time with loved ones, and creating precious memories.

When you want some fun, seek adventure and an experience of life. Check out a museum, visit an art gallery, or attend a special community program. Invest in education or travel that broadens your perspective. When you want to celebrate a special occasion with a loved one, share a fun activity together.

acquire

*LORD, let me know my end, and what is the measure of my days; let me know how fleeting my life is.*

Psalm 39:4 NRSV

>> Plan your next vacation around enjoying an adventure in an exciting new location instead of merely lounging by the pool or shopping in tourist traps.

# #92

## Find More Rewarding Work

> *Hard work is a thrill and a joy when you are in the will of God.*
>
> Robert A. Cook

work

When you're happy with your job, you give your full energy to it, and you receive energy and excitement in doing the work. The work becomes its own reward. It's easier on you to do work that you enjoy than to be unhappy at your job.

Ask God to show you what simple steps you can take to either make the job you're in more fulfilling or to find more rewarding work. Don't underestimate your ability to create the life you desire. Look for ways to improve or expand your skills, or update your résumé and look for a new job.

>> Invest in yourself by doing something you love, whether you are paid for it or not. A well-developed skill can open unexpected doors of opportunity.

# #93

## Make Home Cozy

Home is where you nurture your soul and rest your body. Make your home a simple refuge from the busy world, a place where you can relax and be yourself. A cozy, welcoming home offers shelter from the storms of life.

You don't need a mansion or expensive furnishings. Simple details, like a comfortable chair and a good reading lamp, a few fine pictures on the wall, or a colorful bedspread and some curtains make home cozy and welcoming. All it takes is some imagination and ingenuity—and a little love—to create a living space that you want to come home to.

cozy

*Strength of character may be acquired at work, but beauty of character is learned at home. There the affections are trained. There the gentle life reaches us, the true heaven life.*

Henry Drummond

≫ Display family pictures and memorabilia creatively in collages and on bulletin boards as well as in the usual frames.

# #94

## Cultivate a Sense of Community

> *Rejoice with those who rejoice, and weep with those who weep. Be of the same mind toward one another.*
>
> Romans 12:15–16
> NKJV

cultivate

One of the sweetest pleasures of simple living is being with friends and loved ones. Cultivating community keeps you in touch with the old-fashioned graces of Sunday dinners, porch parties, and gatherings with friends. Having a network of friends and neighbors creates an emotional support system that benefits everyone.

It doesn't take much to celebrate life together. Welcome your new neighbor with fresh muffins in a basket. Call a few friends over for a potluck. Meet a friend for tea on a regular basis. Connect with loved ones far away by letter or e-mail. Pitch in to help a local church or community organization.

≫ Reach out to a friend for mutual support. Meet on a regular basis to encourage and help each other in practical ways.

# #95

## Have Faith in the Process

Sometimes you just have to keep the faith, baby. You may not be able to figure it all out. It's simpler to place it in God's hands and trust the process. Let things unfold as they will, and allow God to lead you every step of the way.

An artist may have a general idea of what he or she wants to create on canvas. Yet sometimes a mistake becomes part of the process that creates a much more interesting painting. You are the artist of your life. So relax and trust the process, and improvise freely, knowing that you are creating a beautiful life.

process

> *It pays to take life seriously; things work out when you trust in GOD.*
>
> Proverbs 16:20 MSG

≫ Write in your journal about a problem that was resolved in an unexpected way, and how the solution was revealed through the process.

focus

# 101 ways to

renew

brainstorm

create

sleep in

# simplify your life

start

respect

nurture

# #96

## Live Your Ideals

> *Far away there in the sunshine are my highest aspirations. I may not reach them, but I can look up and see their beauty, believe in them, and try to follow where they lead.*
>
> Louisa May Alcott

ideals

You may not be able to live out your ideals perfectly, but staying true to them nurtures your soul and makes you feel closer to heaven. Creating a simpler life means making moral and spiritual choices that are meaningful to you and true to what you believe.

You'll be at peace with yourself when you keep faith with what's most important to you. Ask God to help you with decisions, especially when it comes to standing for the truth. He'll give you the wisdom and strength to do your best, and the understanding to forgive yourself when you fall short of your highest ideals.

>> Think about the choices you made today. What were your motives for doing what you did? Would you make the same choices again?

# #97

## Be an Independent Thinker

Think for yourself. Going along with the crowd can seem easy at first, but it may lead you down a wrong road. Know yourself. It's simpler to live by your own convictions than to imitate someone else's style.

God gave you a good mind. Use it. Be an independent thinker who is willing to choose simple values over sophisticated arguments. Choose the company you want to keep, and spend your energies on what's most important to you. Ignorance is costly. Educate yourself on issues so you'll have an informed opinion and make wiser decisions.

thinker

> *Our life is what our thoughts make it.*
>
> Saint Catherine of Siena

>> Monitor news and entertainment choices. Choose only those programs that inform and contribute to a higher quality of life.

# #98
## Be Generous

> *All goes well for those who are generous, who lend freely and conduct their business fairly. Such people will not be overcome by evil circumstances. Those who are righteous will be long remembered.*
>
> Psalm 112:5–6 NLT

generous

Generosity is a way of thinking and looking at life situations. When you have a generous attitude, you are willing to think the best of others and give them the benefit of the doubt, even when you disagree with them. You reflect God's generosity and forgiveness. You believe that God can work all things together for good. An openhanded and open-hearted generosity allows room for God to work in any situation.

A generous person lives from the heart and is willing to share resources with others: time, energy, finances, and love. A pinched attitude closes off resources; a generous attitude allows simple abundance to flow freely.

≫ Express your generosity through simple acts of kindness. Pay for a friend's meal. Give a love offering of time or money or personal service.

# #99

## Hold Things Lightly

The river of time is ever changing, constantly moving. Though you may wish to hold on to a certain season of your life, the seasons change. When you understand that everything is a gift from God, you can hold each changing moment with an open hand, knowing that just as he filled your hand once, he can fill it again with something new.

Hold things lightly instead of clutching them tightly. A clenched fist grows stiff and tired from holding on, while an open hand is able to give and receive freely. Allowing the ebb and flow to move easily creates room for grace to enter.

hold

*Live near to God, and so all things will appear to you little in comparison with eternal realities.*

Robert Murray M'Cheyne

≫ Remember that you are a child of God, and open your hands in praise and worship, thanking him that this life contains the seeds of eternal life.

# #100

## Be a Creator, Not a Consumer

*We are His workmanship, created in Christ Jesus for good works, which God prepared beforehand that we should walk in them.*

Ephesians 2:10 NKJV

create

God has placed you here on this earth, at this time, because you have a unique contribution to offer. Your choices are important. You put more of your energy into creating instead of consuming when you choose a simpler life. Rather than defining yourself by what you own, you define yourself by acts of mercy and kindness, and by becoming the person God created.

Live creatively by nurturing your gifts and talents. Instead of consuming the world's resources, seek to contribute to the good of all. Trust that God will guide you as you learn to reflect his creativity in your world.

≫ Nurture and encourage the creativity of the next generation by sharing a skill you have developed or by empathizing with their hopes and dreams.

# #101

## Practice Spiritual Simplicity

The simplicity of paring down, cleaning out, and clearing clutter in your physical life can be a reflection of an inner simplicity that is deeply rooted in God. This inner spiritual simplicity can be described as a childlike faith in the One who created you and who is with you every single day of your life.

Resting in the greatness and grace of God frees you to make the elegant choices that will transform your life from one of anxiety and chaos to a life filled with an abundance of joy and peace. When you focus on the essentials, all else will fall into place.

simplicity

*The serene silent beauty of a holy life is the most powerful influence in the world, next to the might of the Spirit of God.*

Blaise Pascal

≫ Write a personal purpose statement to gain insight into the spiritual qualities you want to cultivate in your life.

*Making the simple complicated is commonplace; making the complicated simple, awesomely simple, that's creativity.*

Charles Mingus

*Jesus said, "I've come to change everything, turn everything rightside up."*

Luke 12:50 MSG